HOCKEY TRIVIA for kids

Eric Zweig

Scholastic Canada Ltd.
604 King Street West, Toronto, Ontario M5V 1E1, Canada

Scholastic Inc.
557 Broadway, New York, NY 10012, USA

Scholastic Australia Pty Limited
PO Box 579, Gosford, NSW 2250, Australia

Scholastic New Zealand Limited
Private Bag 94407, Greenmount, Auckland, New Zealand

Scholastic Children's Books
Euston House, 24 Eversholt Street, London NW1 1DB, UK

Photo Credits:
Cover: Dave Sandford/Getty Images;
p. 1: Courtesy © Bank of Canada; bank note image used with permission;
p. 3: Doug MacLellan/Hockey Hall of Fame; p. 14: Paul Bereswill/Hockey Hall of Fame;
p. 25: Dave Sandford/Hockey Canada/HHOF; p. 36: London Life-Portnoy/Hockey Hall of Fame;
p. 41: Dave Sandford/Hockey Hall of Fame; p. 42: Imperial Oil-Turofsky/Hockey Hall of Fame;
p. 46: Imperial Oil-Turofsky/Hockey Hall of Fame; p. 64: Imperial Oil-Turofsky/Hockey Hall of
Fame; p. 72: Paul Bereswill/Hockey Hall of Fame; p. 75: Dave Sandford/Hockey Hall of Fame;
p. 88: Paul Bereswill/Hockey Hall of Fame; p. 106: Fred Keenan/Hockey Hall of Fame;
p. 107: Doug MacLellan/Hockey Hall of Fame; p. 115: Dave Sandford/Hockey Hall of Fame;
p. 118: Hockey Hall of Fame; p. 121: Frank Lennon/Toronto Star

Library and Archives Canada Cataloguing in Publication
Zweig, Eric, 1963-
Hockey trivia for kids / Eric Zweig.
ISBN 0-439-95266-2
1. Hockey--Miscellanea--Juvenile literature.
2. National Hockey League--Miscellanea--Juvenile literature. I. Title.
GV847.25.Z94 2006   j796.962   C2006-901216-4

6 5 4 3 2 1   Printed in Canada   06 07 08 09 10

To Amanda, even though she likes baseball better.
— *Eric*

INTRODUCTION

Canadians love hockey. Many people have tried to explain just why it is that we love it so much. There are some who say it's because of our rugged pioneer roots. Others say it's because Canada is a land of ice and snow. Maybe those theories are right. But I think the answer is much simpler than that: Canadians love hockey because hockey is fun! It's fun to play and it's fun to watch.

Most of us will never be NHL players, or represent our country at the Olympics, but that doesn't mean we can't have fun playing hockey, and it doesn't mean we can't dream about doing it. Reading stories about people who've played a part in our national sport helps to fuel our imaginations. Whether it's a story about a great player or about an invention that made the game better, reading about hockey is lots of fun too.

When I was ten years old, my teacher would scold me for filling my current events book with so many sports stories. Today, I get to make my living writing about sports and looking up stories about hockey players. I wasn't good enough to be an NHL player, so I'm pretty lucky that I still get to make my living in hockey. I hope Mrs. Howchin would agree.

Five and Nine

We all know that the front of the Canadian five-dollar bill features a portrait of Sir Wilfrid Laurier, who served as prime minister from 1896 to 1911. But have you ever taken a close look at the back of the five-dollar bill? It's as Canadian as you can get.

On the back is a picture of children sledding, skating and playing hockey. There is also a quotation from Roch Carrier's well-known short story, *The Hockey Sweater*, about a boy growing up in Quebec in the 1940s, who, instead of getting a new Montreal Canadiens sweater to wear like his hero Maurice Richard, is sent a Toronto Maple Leafs sweater. And if you know your hockey history, you'll notice that a child on the ice is wearing a sweater with the number 9 — a tribute to Maurice "Rocket" Richard.

Lord Stanley's Cup

Like hockey itself, the Stanley Cup is a lot older than the NHL. Teams have been competing for it since 1893.

Lord Frederick Arthur Stanley, the Earl of Preston, is the man behind the Stanley Cup. He was born in London, England, and served as the Governor General of Canada from 1888 to 1893. Lord Stanley was a fan of many sports, but he had never seen a hockey game until he came to Canada.

On March 18, 1892, Lord Stanley announced that he was going to donate a championship trophy for hockey "considering the general interest which matches now elicit," which is just a fancy way of saying because it was very popular. The trophy was presented for the first time in 1893 to the Montreal Hockey Club, a team belonging to the Montreal Amateur Athletic Association. In the early days, many different teams in many different leagues were all trying to win the Stanley Cup. Today, of course, the trophy goes to the championship team in the National Hockey League. In fact, since 1927, the NHL has been the only league that has been allowed to compete for the Cup.

The original Stanley Cup

The shortest overtime period in NHL playoff history lasted only nine seconds. Brian Skrudland of the Montreal Canadiens scored against Mike Vernon of the Calgary Flames on May 18, 1986.

CUP CAPERS

Back in 1893, the Stanley Cup was a lot smaller than it is now. The original Cup — which can be seen at the Hockey Hall of Fame in Toronto — was only the size of the bowl that sits on top of the trophy today. Over the years, the Cup has grown in both size and stature . . . but it hasn't always been treated as kindly as it should.

According to legend, following their 1905 Cup win, some of the Ottawa Silver Seven players wondered if anyone could kick it across the Rideau Canal. The Cup was lined up and booted . . . but it didn't make it. The Cup landed in the middle of the canal. Fortunately, the water was frozen, so it didn't sink. Still, the Cup sat there all night until it could be rescued the next day.

DID YOU KNOW?

Early radio and TV broadcasts of NHL games always came on the air well after the game had started. This was because team owners were worried that people wouldn't buy tickets if they could listen to or watch the games for free. Hockey Night in Canada didn't show a whole game on TV until the 1968–69 season — its 16th.

The Great Debate

There's no denying it: hockey is Canada's game. We play it on ice. We play it on asphalt. We play it on tabletops and on video screens. There are more boys and girls registered to play minor hockey in Canada than there are anywhere else in the world. We've been playing it for a long time, and we're fiercely proud of it. But just where did it get its start?

Hockey has been around for hundreds of years. The first skates were made from bones or antlers that were tied with laces to the skater's footwear. Metal blades were eventually attached to the skater's boots with straps and buckles, or screwed right to the bottom of the boot. But exactly where hockey as we know it began is one of the most debated issues in sports.

The biggest debate is probably whether hockey got its start in Windsor, Nova Scotia, in the early 1800s, or Kingston, Ontario, in the mid-1800s. Early stories have soldiers playing on-ice versions of the games they had played at home in England, Scotland and Ireland which they called ice rugby, ice polo, ice hurley or ice hockey.

But one of the earliest mentions of the word "hockey" is from October 25, 1825. In a letter to a friend, explorer Sir John Franklin explains how he and his men skated and played a game they called hockey on a small lake in what is now Deline in the Northwest Territories.

A Brave New Game

The credit for making hockey so popular should go to James Creighton. In 1872, Creighton, who had played early games on ice while he was growing up in Halifax, Nova Scotia, moved to Montreal. His new friends, who already knew how to skate, were fascinated with this Nova Scotia game. They asked Creighton to write down a set of rules.

Creighton borrowed heavily from the game of rugby. Forward passing was not permitted. The ball had to be passed backward or sideways. (Later, the top and bottom would be cut off the ball to keep it from bouncing over the boards around the rink.

This was the first hockey puck.) There were nine players on each side, as well as one referee and two goal judges. The goal judges had to be especially

brave — they stood right on the ice behind and between the goal posts. There wasn't a net or a crossbar, just two posts sticking up from the ice.

Then, on March 3, 1875, the Montreal *Gazette* reported that "a game of hockey" was to be played that evening at the Victoria Skating Rink. A new sport was born.

Today — more than 130 years later — the game you play on your local rink and the game played in packed NHL arenas is the direct descendant of the game once played by James Creighton and his friends in Montreal.

Captain Fantastic

Steve Yzerman was made captain of the Detroit Red Wings for the 1986–87 season. At the time, he was just 21 years old. That made him the youngest captain in Red Wings history. He since has gone on to become the longest-serving captain in NHL history — the 2005–06 season marked Yzerman's 20th year as Red Wings captain.

Law of the Land

Is hockey really Canada's game? You bet. On May 12, 1994, a bill passed by the Canadian government became a law. Bill C-212 officially declared hockey as Canada's National Winter Sport.

DID YOU KNOW?

The NHL is pretty particular about what goes on the ice. According to NHL rules, a hockey puck must be one inch thick with a three-inch diameter, and each puck must weigh between five-and-a-half and six ounces (156 and 170 grams). And even though a puck is 90% rubber, it's actually made up of about a dozen different ingredients. Either coal dust or carbon black is used as filler, which also give pucks their black colour. Other additives, such as sulphur, help strengthen it. In Glas Co in Sherbrooke, Quebec, makes all NHL pucks.

Will it Never End?

The longest game in NHL history was played on March 24, 1936, between the Detroit Red Wings and the Montreal Maroons. Detroit and Montreal were scoreless until the sixth overtime period! Finally, after 116:30 of extra play, Mud Bruneteau gave Detroit a 1–0 victory. Bruneteau scored his winning goal against Maroons goalie Lorne Chabot.

BY THE NUMBERS

NHL Team	Stanley Cup wins
Montreal Canadiens	24*
Toronto Maple Leafs	13^
Detroit Red Wings	10
Boston Bruins	5
Edmonton Oilers	5
New York Rangers	4
New York Islanders	4
Chicago Blackhawks	3
New Jersey Devils	3
Philadelphia Flyers	2
Pittsburgh Penguins	2
Colorado Avalanche	2

NHL Team   Stanley Cup wins

Dallas Stars 1

Calgary Flames 1

Tampa Bay Lightning 1

Carolina Hurricanes 1

*Montreal's Stanley Cup wins include a victory in 1916, before the NHL was formed

^Toronto's Stanley Cup wins include victories by the Arenas in 1918 and the St. Pats in 1922, but not a victory by the Toronto Blueshirts in 1914, before the NHL was formed

Octopus's Garden

There's an unusual tradition in Detroit that has been going on for more than 50 years: throwing an octopus onto the ice at Red Wings games, especially during the playoffs.

This strange tradition began back in 1952. At

A linesman cleans up during a Detroit game.

the time, there were only two rounds of playoffs in the NHL. That meant it took eight victories to win the Stanley Cup. Each tentacle of the octopus was symbolic of a win needed in the playoffs. Brothers Pete and Jerry Cusimano — who owned a local fish market — snuck a dead octopus into the Detroit Olympia arena for a playoff game on April 15, 1952. Pete tossed it onto the ice during the second period. The Red Wings beat the Canadiens that night to win the Stanley Cup with their eighth straight win in the playoffs. The octopus has been a good luck charm in Detroit ever since.

DID YOU KNOW?

According to David Keon, who works for the NHL public relations department in Toronto, 36 pucks are put in the freezer before a game at the Air Canada Centre. Usually it takes a dozen pucks to get through an average NHL game.

When One Was Enough

When the Los Angeles Kings played the Minnesota North Stars on November 10, 1979, the puck they were using was never shot into the stands. They played the whole game with just one puck, which is on display at the Hockey Hall of Fame in Toronto.

DID YOU KNOW?

Arthur Farrell, who played for the Montreal Shamrocks, wrote the very first hockey book — way back in 1899. It's called Hockey: Canada's Royal Winter Game. *Only three copies are known to exist.*

Out of This World

Not only is hockey an international game, but it's getting its start in space too. In October 1984 Dr. Marc Garneau, Canada's first astronaut, blasted into space aboard the shuttle *Challenger*. He carried a puck with him, which was later used in the ceremonial face-off for the 1985 All-Star Game in Calgary.

A Puck By Any Other Name

Ever wonder why we call a puck a puck?
Some think it comes from Shakespeare's play
A Midsummer Night's Dream. In it, Puck, a
mischievous sprite, appears and disappears
without warning — sort of like a hockey puck
in a crowd of sticks and skates.

More likely, though, the word comes from an
Irish game called hurling, which is a mixture of
field hockey and lacrosse. In Irish slang, the word
"puck" is sometimes used to mean smack or strike.
For example, "a puck in the puss" is like saying a
punch in the mouth.

BY THE NUMBERS

Here is a history of NHL teams:

NHL Team	Franchise Date	First Season
Montreal Canadiens	November 26, 1917	1917–18
Toronto Maple Leafs*	November 26, 1917	1917–18
Boston Bruins	November 1, 1924	1924–25
New York Rangers	May 15, 1926	1926–27
Chicago Blackhawks	September 25, 1926	1926–27
Detroit Red Wings**	September 25, 1926	1926–27
Dallas Stars***	June 5, 1967	1967–68
Los Angeles Kings	June 5, 1967	1967–68
Philadelphia Flyers	June 5, 1967	1967–68
Pittsburgh Penguins	June 5, 1967	1967–68

NHL Team	Franchise Date	First Season
St. Louis Blues	June 5, 1967	1967–68
Buffalo Sabres	May 22, 1970	1970–71
Vancouver Canucks	May 22, 1970	1970–71
Calgary Flames^	June 6, 1972	1972–73
New York Islanders	June 6, 1972	1972–73
New Jersey Devils^^	June 11, 1974	1974–75
Washington Capitals	June 11, 1974	1974–75
Colorado Avalanche^^^	June 22, 1979	1979–80
Edmonton Oilers	June 22, 1979	1979–80
Phoenix Coyotes°	June 22, 1979	1979–80
Carolina Hurricanes°°	June 22, 1979	1979–80
San Jose Sharks	May 9, 1990	1991–92
Ottawa Senators	December 16, 1991	1992–93

NHL Team	Franchise Date	First Season
Tampa Bay Lightning	December 16, 1991	1992–93
Florida Panthers	June 14, 1993	1993–94
Mighty Ducks of Anaheim	June 15, 1993	1993–94
Nashville Predators	June 25, 1997	1998–99
Atlanta Thrashers	June 25, 1997	1999–00
Columbus Blue Jackets	June 25, 1997	2000–01
Minnesota Wild	June 25, 1997	2000–01

*team name became Maple Leafs in February 1927
**team name became Red Wings in 1932–33
***transferred from Minnesota to Dallas on June 9, 1993
^transferred from Atlanta to Calgary on June 24, 1980
^^transferred from Kansas City to Denver, then from
    Denver to New Jersey on June 30, 1982
^^^transferred from Quebec to Colorado on June 21, 1995
°transferred from Winnipeg to Phoenix on July 1, 1996
°°transferred from Hartford to Carolina on June 25, 1997

NAME GAME

The name Canadiens was chosen for Montreal's team to represent the French-speaking people of Quebec, who called themselves *canadiens*. Sometimes people refer to the Canadiens as the "Habs." According to stories, this nickname dates back to 1924. Tex Rickard, who owned Madison Square Garden in New York, was told that the "H" on the Canadiens sweater stood for *habitant*, a French word that was once used to describe the farmers of Quebec. Rickard was told that the French players on the team came from farms and that they were therefore "habitants" or "habs." Really, though, the "H" on the sweater stands for "hockey." The Montreal Canadiens' official name is le Club de Hockey Canadien.

DID YOU KNOW?

The 1993 playoffs featured more overtime games than any season in NHL history. Of the 85 games played that spring, 28 went into overtime.

CUP CAPERS

Bob Nystrom's overtime goal in 1980 gave the New York Islanders their first of four straight Stanley Cup Championships. After they won, teammate Clark Gillies let his dog eat out of the Stanley Cup bowl. When asked to explain, Gillies simply said, "Hey, he's a nice dog."

DID YOU KNOW?

The last non-NHL team to win the Stanley Cup was the Victoria Cougars, in 1925. The Cougars, who played in the Western Hockey League, beat the Montreal Canadiens.

Wicked-heiser

Haley Wickenheiser is considered to be one of the best women's hockey players in the world. Wickenheiser first joined the Canadian women's national team in 1994 when she was just 15 years old. She played hockey at the Winter Olympics in 1998, 2002 and 2006 and was also a member of the Canadian women's softball team at the 2000 Summer Olympics in Sydney, Australia, making her the first woman to represent Canada at both the Summer and the Winter Olympic Games.

In 1998 Wickenheiser attended a training camp for Philadelphia Flyers rookies. In 2003 she joined a men's hockey team in Finland and scored her first goal for Kirkkonummi Salamat on January 11, 2003. That made her the first woman to score a goal in a men's professional hockey league.

Haley Wickenheiser after her gold medal win

NAME GAME

When a new Ottawa expansion team joined the NHL in 1991, it took the name of the old Ottawa team that had played in the league from 1917 to 1934. That name, of course, is the Ottawa Senators.

Hat Trick

When a player scores three goals in a game, fans will often throw hats onto the ice. That's because scoring three goals in a game is known as a hat trick. In fact, doing three of almost anything in sports these days is often referred to as a hat trick. But where does the term come from?

Hat trick actually comes from the English game of cricket. It refers to a bowler who takes three wickets with three straight balls. (A bowler is like the pitcher in baseball. Taking three straight wickets is like striking out three straight batters. In cricket, this is very rare.)

Apparently, back in the 1800s, it was the custom that if a bowler could take three straight wickets in three successive balls, his team would buy him a new hat. Some people tell the story a bit differently, though. They say that if the bowler achieved this impressive feat, he would pass his hat around the stands and fans would fill it with money.

It's often said that Sammy Taft brought the term to hockey in the 1940s. Taft lived in Toronto and sold hats from a store on Spadina Avenue. When a player scored three goals in a game at Maple Leaf Gardens, he would give the player a free hat.

Taft certainly did a lot to make it a popular term, but the truth is people had been referring to three goals as a hat trick in hockey since at least the 1920s. On December 26, 1930, legendary sportswriter Michael J. Rodden wrote this in his column about a New York Rangers game: "Bunny Cook had a field day, getting three consecutive goals to perform the hat trick deluxe."

Uphill Battle

Al Hill holds the record for most points by a player in his first NHL game. Hill was called up to the Philadelphia Flyers on February 14, 1977. He had five points that night: two goals and three assists. He played only eight more games for the Flyers that year and added only one more assist.

Not So Original Six

When people talk about the old days of the NHL, they often talk about the "Original Six." That's because for many years there were only six teams in the league. The Original Six are: the Montreal Canadiens, Toronto Maple Leafs, Boston Bruins, New York Rangers, Chicago Blackhawks and Detroit Red Wings.

Really, though, most of the Original Six teams aren't original at all!

When the NHL was formed in 1917, it actually had five teams: the Montreal Canadiens, Montreal Wanderers, Toronto Arenas, Ottawa Senators and Quebec Bulldogs. The Quebec team didn't have enough money to start right away, and the Wanderers had to drop out of the league early because their arena burned down. So, in a way, Montreal, Toronto and Ottawa were the NHL's Original Three.

By the end of the 1920s, the NHL had grown from three teams to ten. In addition to Toronto, Montreal and Ottawa, there were now seven others: the Montreal Maroons, Boston Bruins, Detroit Cougars, Chicago Black Hawks, New York Rangers, New York Americans and Pittsburgh Pirates.

Then the 1930s came along. Times were tough because of the Great Depression, and many teams were losing money. The NHL began to lose some of its teams. The teams from both Pittsburgh and Ottawa had to move. Pittsburgh became the Philadelphia Quakers. Ottawa became the St. Louis Eagles. Still, the teams lost money and soon, both went out of business, followed by the Montreal

Maroons and the New York Americans. By 1942 the NHL was left with just six teams: the so-called Original Six. They remained the only teams in the league until 1967.

CUP CAPERS

Though they only lasted a few weeks in the NHL, the Montreal Wanderers had once been the top team in hockey. The team was a Stanley Cup champion in 1906, 1907, 1908 and 1910. But they weren't always the best keepers of the Cup.

According to hockey legend, the Wanderers once forgot all about the coveted trophy. They left it at a photographer's studio after having their team picture taken in 1907. A woman working in the studio found it and thought the Cup would make a lovely flowerpot. She used it to hold flowers for several months before someone from the Wanderers finally came back to claim it!

When the Wanderers won the Cup again in 1910, one of the players put it on display at a bowling alley he owned in Montreal. He filled the Cup with packs of gum, which he then sold to his customers.

America's Cup

Though the Bruins were the first American team in the NHL, they weren't the first team from the United States to play for the Stanley Cup. In 1916 the Portland Rosebuds, from the state of Oregon, faced the Montreal Canadiens. They lost. In 1917 the Seattle Metropolitans, from Washington State, faced the Canadiens and became the first U.S.-based team to win the Cup.

Even though Seattle is an American city, every player on the Metropolitans' roster was a Canadian. All but one Portland player in 1916 were Canadian too.

Can I Help You?

Wayne Gretzky retired as an NHL player in 1999. At that time, he held or shared 61 different NHL records. Even though he still holds the NHL records for most goals in a season and most goals in a career, Gretzky never really considered himself to

be a great scorer — really! He was most proud
of his skill as a playmaker: he liked to help his
teammates score. In his career, Gretzky had 1,963
assists. That's more than anyone else in NHL
history. Not only that, it means Gretzky has more
assists than any other player has total points!

Locked Out

As the NHL expanded during the 1990s, so too
did players' salaries. Then, due to disagreements
about how much money the players should be
paid, in 2004–05 the NHL became the first major
professional sports league to cancel a whole season.
Money wasn't the only issue, but it was the most
important one. The NHL owners wanted players'
salaries to be linked to the money that the league
made. That meant players would only earn a
certain percentage of the money the league made.
The players called it a "salary cap," and they didn't
want one.

Because of the disagreement between the

players and owners, a lockout began at midnight on September 15, 2004. That meant that no games would be played until the players and owners reached an agreement. Many people feared that the lockout might last longer than one season. Fortunately it didn't. On July 13, 2005, a new, six-year agreement was reached.

The new NHL season began on October 5, 2005, with 15 games on the schedule. That meant that it was the first time that all 30 teams had played on the same night.

The biggest crowd anywhere in the NHL that night was in Tampa Bay. The arena there is only supposed to hold 19,758 people, but the crowd reached 22,120. The Lightning had won the Stanley Cup in 2004, but because of the lockout, fans in Tampa Bay had been forced to wait more than a year to watch their team raise their championship banner.

NAME GAME

When the New York Rangers joined the NHL in 1926, they were owned by Tex Rickard, who owned Madison Square Garden. Since the state of Texas has a police force known as the Texas Rangers, Rickard wanted the team to be known as "Tex's Rangers," and the name stuck.

Red Wings, Grey Hair

Gordie Howe had the longest career in professional hockey history — 32 years!

For 25 years, he played with the Detroit Red Wings. But after the 1970–71 season, he retired. He must have missed it pretty badly, because two years later, he once again took to the ice. A new league, the World Hockey Association (WHA), had formed, and the Houston Aeros signed Gordie's sons, Mark and Marty. Even though Gordie was 45 years old, he decided to join his sons on the ice.

Gordie and his sons played six seasons together in the new league. Then, in 1979–80, four teams from the WHA joined the NHL. Gordie was 51 years old. That season he played all 80 games, and scored 15 goals, in what would end up being his final season in the NHL.

Some players have come close, but no one has ever matched Gordie Howe's 26 seasons in the NHL, or his 1,767 games. Only Wayne Gretzky has more than his 801 NHL goals. And when his WHA totals are included, Gordie played for 32 years and in 2,186 games, scoring 975 goals. Not bad for a grandfather.

Howe in his last season with Detroit

NAME GAME

When Detroit entered the NHL in 1926, the team was known as the Cougars. That's because the franchise had previously been known as the Victoria Cougars. But in 1930, the name was changed to the Detroit Falcons. Since their sweaters were red and white, in 1932, team president James Norris changed the name to the Red Wings.

Norris had grown up in Montreal where he had been a member of the Montreal Amateur Athletic Association, whose sports teams were known as the "Winged Wheelers." Since Detroit is known as the Motor City (because so many cars are built there), Norris thought that their winged wheel logo would be a perfect, fit and put a wheel with a wing on their sweaters.

Since the introduction of the Stanley Cup in 1893, the name of the team that wins the prized mug has always been engraved right onto the trophy. The first team to engrave the names of all its players on the Stanley Cup was the Montreal Wanderers in 1907. Since 1924, every team that has won the Stanley Cup has engraved the names of its players on the trophy, as well as the names of owners, coaches, general managers and other members of the organization. The first woman to have her name engraved on the Stanley Cup was Marguerite Norris. She was the president of the Detroit Red Wings when they won the Cup in 1954 and 1955. In the years since then, the names of about a dozen women have been engraved on the Stanley Cup.

BY THE NUMBERS

Here's a look at the defensemen who have won the Norris Trophy as the league's best defenseman the most times:

Player	Wins
Bobby Orr	8
Doug Harvey	7
Raymond Bourque	5
Nicklas Lidstrom	4
Chris Chelios	3
Paul Coffey	3
Denis Potvin	3
Pierre Pilote	3

CUP CAPERS

Over the years, many mistakes (and some corrections) have been made in the names engraved on the Stanley Cup. Here's a look at some of the strangest:

1937–38: Chicago Blackhawks

Pete Palangio had his name engraved twice. One time, it's spelled correctly. The other time it's spelled P-A-L-A-G-I-O.

1941–42: Toronto Maple Leafs

Maple Leafs goalie Turk Broda is listed twice. One time, he's engraved as TURK BRODA. The other time, his real name of WALTER BRODA appears on the Cup.

1951–52: Detroit Red Wings

Two mistakes were made this year. Coach Tommy Ivan is engraved as TOMMY NIVAN. Alex Delvecchio's last name is misspelled as BELVECCHIO.

1956–1960: Montreal Canadiens

Montreal won the Stanley Cup five years

in a row . . . and Jacques Plante's name is spelled differently each time.

1962–63: Toronto Maple Leafs

The team name is misspelled as TORONTO MAPLE LEAES

1971–72: Boston Bruins

Misspelled as BQSTQN BRUINS.

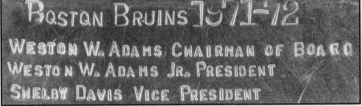

One of the errors on the Cup

1980–81: New York Islanders

Misspelled as NEW YORK ILANDERS.

1995–96: Colorado Avalanche

Adam Deadmarsh was misspelled as ADAM DEADMARCH. Later, this mistake was corrected. It was the first time a correction was made to a misspelled name on the Stanley Cup.

2001–02: Detroit Red Wings

MANNY LAGACE was corrected to MANNY LEGACE.

DID YOU KNOW?

In 1944–45 Montreal Canadiens legend Maurice "Rocket" Richard was the first player in NHL history to score 50 goals in a single season. Richard was also the first player in NHL history to score 500 goals in his career. He accomplished that feat on October 19, 1957. Both marks remain important milestones in the career of any great NHL scorer.

Richard eyes the goal.

Saint Patrick

As an NHL rookie in 1985–86, Patrick Roy seemed to be a bundle of nerves. His head was constantly bobbing up and down as he craned his neck from side to side. Roy even admitted that he sometimes liked to talk to his goal posts!

Roy may have looked strange, but he was good — especially in the playoffs. Montreal wasn't expected to go very far that year, but Roy led the Canadiens all the way to the Stanley Cup. And in 1993 his performance was even more amazing.

After losing the opening game of the 1993 playoffs in overtime, Roy promised his teammates that he wouldn't surrender another overtime goal that year. And he didn't. The Canadiens played ten more overtime games that spring and won them all. Until then, no NHL team had ever won more than six overtime games. Three of Roy's victories came in the Finals, where the Canadiens defeated the Los Angeles Kings to win the Stanley Cup once again.

"When Patrick makes a promise, he keeps it," said teammate Mike Keane. "He said he was going to shut the door, and he did."

CUP CAPERS

Following the Canadiens' Stanley Cup celebration in 1924, team owner Leo Dandurand invited the players over to his house for a victory party. There, they would drink from the famous silver bowl. After the game some players grabbed the Cup and climbed into a car to head over to his house. Along the way, though, they got a flat tire. While the boys got out to make their repairs, they put the

SNIFF SNIFF

Cup on the curb beside them. When they finally arrived at Dandurand's house and got ready to take their drink, they discovered that they had left the Stanley Cup behind! So they piled back into the car and drove back through the streets of Montreal. Luckily for them, they found the Cup right where they had left it, sitting on the curb.

The Last Goal He Ever Scored

Toronto hockey fans loved Bill Barilko. He was a solid defenseman who was as handsome as he was hard-hitting. In five seasons with the Maple Leafs, from 1946–47 to 1950–51, he helped Toronto win the Stanley Cup four times. The Cup Final in 1951 was one of the most thrilling in hockey history. Each of the five games played by Toronto and the Montreal Canadiens went into overtime.

Leafs coach Joe Primeau had told Barilko to concentrate on defense. He didn't want him jumping into the offensive zone. Yet at 2:53 of overtime in Game Five, Barilko raced in from the Montreal blue line. He dove at the puck and chopped it toward the net. Barilko's shot went in, and the Leafs won the Stanley Cup! Sadly, it was the last goal he ever scored.

Bill Barilko disappeared that summer. He was on a fishing trip when his plane crashed in the woods of northern Ontario. The Maple Leafs didn't win

Barilko, the 1951 Stanley Cup hero

the Stanley Cup again until 1962. By strange coincidence, that was the same year that Barilko's remains were finally discovered.

Scoring is an Art

The NHL's scoring leader — the player who gets the most points, which includes goals and assists — is awarded the Art Ross Trophy. Strangely, Art Ross himself only had one point in his entire NHL career. Of course, he only played three games! Ross was a star defenseman who played most of his career before the NHL was formed. Later, he became the first coach and general manager of the Boston Bruins.

Ross planned to donate a trophy to the NHL in 1941. He wanted his trophy to go the NHL's most outstanding player. But the NHL already had the Hart Trophy, which goes to the Most Valuable Player during the regular NHL season. Instead, it was decided that Ross's trophy would be used to reward the NHL's scoring leader. It was first presented to Elmer Lach in 1948.

Boom Boom and Bobby

Hockey's next 50-goals-in-a-season scorer after Maurice Richard was also a member of the Montreal Canadiens. Bernie "Boom Boom" Geoffrion reached the milestone in 1960–61. His nickname was "Boom Boom" because when he took a shot — boom! It was powerful.

But Bobby Hull also had a powerful shot. Hull played for the Chicago Blackhawks, and one year after Geoffrion scored his 50 goals, Hull made it to 50 too — on the final night of the 1961–62 season.

Four years later, Hull scored his 50th goal of the season after Chicago had played just 57 games. That meant Hull had 13 more games to become the first player in NHL history to score more than 50 goals in one season. It seemed like a cinch. But it wasn't.

Over the next five days, Hull couldn't score a single goal. Not only that, no one on the Blackhawks could score. Chicago was shut out for three straight games! Finally, on March 12, 1966, Hull blasted a shot past Cesar Maniago of the New York Rangers. The new goal-scoring record was his. He scored three more times before the year was over, and ended the 1965–66 season with 54 goals. Hull also won the Art Ross Trophy that year. His 54 goals plus 43 assists gave him 97 points, which also set an NHL record.

DID YOU KNOW?

Manon Rheaume was a goalie who helped the Canadian women's national team win the World Championship in 1992. That year she also became the first woman to play major junior hockey in Canada. She played one game for Trois-Rivières in the Quebec Major Junior Hockey League. Then, on September 23, 1992, Manon Rheaume became the first woman to play in the NHL. She played for the Tampa Bay Lightning in a pre-season game against the St. Louis Blues.

Rinks Rule

The very first rule in the NHL rulebook is about the ice and is called quite simply "Rink." Here's what it says: "The game of 'Ice Hockey' shall be played on an ice surface known as the 'RINK.'"

No rink dimensions were included as part of the NHL Official Rules until 1929–30. That season, they were officially made 200 feet by 85 feet. This was the size of the ice surface at the Victoria Skating Rink in Montreal where the first game of modern hockey was played on March 3, 1875. These dimensions are still used today.

CUP CAPERS

Bobby Hull joined the Chicago Blackhawks for the 1957–58 season. At the time, Chicago was the worst team in the NHL. The league only had six teams, and Chicago had finished sixth nine times in the last eleven years. They missed the playoffs eleven times in twelve years. But, with players like Bobby Hull, Stan Mikita and Glenn Hall, the Blackhawks improved quickly. In 1961 they finally won the Stanley Cup — for the first time since 1938.

Chicago's Stanley Cup victory ended a streak of five championships by the Montreal Canadiens. In fact, Chicago had beaten the Canadiens in the semifinals before winning the Stanley Cup in a series against Detroit. Then, in 1962, Chicago and Montreal met in the semifinals for a second straight year. The Blackhawks won again.

During the 1962 semifinals, the Stanley Cup was on display in the lobby of the Chicago Stadium. A Canadiens fan broke into the display case and tried to steal it, but was quickly caught. His excuse? He couldn't stand a second straight season without seeing the Stanley Cup in Montreal.

Stolen Silverware

A Toronto policeman named Harold "Lumpy" Lambert made one of the biggest saves in hockey history back in 1969. Thieves had stolen three of the NHL's trophies from the Hockey Hall of Fame: the Hart, Conn Smythe and Calder. After tough detective work, Lambert found them wrapped in green garbage bags near a prison outside Toronto.

DID YOU KNOW?

Art Ross was the first coach in NHL history to pull his goalie for an extra attacker. Ross did it on March 26, 1931, during a semifinal playoff series. His Boston Bruins lost the game 1–0 to the Montreal Canadiens.

You Gotta Have Hart

The Hart Trophy, which honours the player who is "adjudged to be the most valuable to his team," is the NHL's oldest individual award. Dr. David Hart donated it in 1923. His son, Cecil Hart, was an executive with the Montreal Canadiens. Frank Nighbor of the Ottawa Senators was the award's first recipient in 1923–24.

Some NHL trophies are awarded by statistics, like the Art Ross Trophy, which goes to the scoring leader, but most trophy winners are selected by a vote. Members of the Professional Hockey Writers Association vote on many of the trophies, but not all of them. For example, the Vezina Trophy, which goes to the league's best goalie, is selected by the general managers of the 30 NHL teams, and the Jack Adams Award for best coach is selected by members of the NHL Broadcasters' Association.

CUP CAPERS

When the Islanders won the Cup in 1980, Bryan Trottier took it home . . . and slept with it! "I wanted to wake up and find it right beside me," Trottier explained. "I didn't want to think I'd just dreamed of this happening."

In a Hart Beat

After the 1999–2000 season, Chris Pronger beat
Jaromir Jagr for the Hart Trophy by a single point
in the voting. At the time, it was the closest vote
in the history of the trophy. However, it got even
closer: two years later Jose Theodore and Jarome
Iginla tied in the voting. Theodore ended up
winning the trophy because he had received more
first-place votes. Iginla didn't go home from the
awards ceremony empty-handed, though. He won
the Maurice Richard Trophy for scoring 52 goals,
and the Art Ross Trophy for collecting 96 points.

DID YOU KNOW?

*Wayne Gretzky is the only player in
NHL history to score more than 200
points in a single season, and he did
it four times! Gretzky had 212
points in 1981–82, 205 points in
1983–84, 208 points in 1984–85
and 215 points in 1985–86.*

Who was that Lady?

The Lady Byng Trophy is the NHL's second-oldest individual award. It was donated to the league in 1925 and rewards sportsmanship and gentlemanly conduct. Lady Byng's full name and title was Marie Moreton, Viscountess  Byng of Vimy. She was married to Julian Byng, Viscount of Vimy, a British general who commanded the Canadian army in World War I. Lady Byng donated her trophy to the NHL while her husband was serving as the Governor General of Canada.

DID YOU KNOW?

The first winner of the Lady Byng Trophy was Ottawa's Frank Nighbor. One year earlier, Nighbor had been the first winner of the Hart Trophy.

A New Set of Six

The NHL officially added six new teams to the "Original Six" on June 5, 1967. The six new teams were the Philadelphia Flyers, Pittsburgh Penguins, St. Louis Blues, Los Angeles Kings, Minnesota North Stars and Oakland Seals.

The NHL now had two divisions. The old six teams played together in the East Division, while the six new teams were in the West Division. The winning team in the East Division played the winning team from the West Division for the Stanley Cup. For the first three seasons, the St. Louis Blues always made it to the Final. They lost the Stanley Cup to Montreal in 1968 and 1969, then lost again to Boston in 1970. In all the years since, the Blues have never made it to the Finals again.

Flying Fast

In 1974 the Philadelphia Flyers were the first of the 1967 expansion teams to win the Stanley Cup. It had only taken them seven seasons to do it, and they followed up that win with another the following year.

Rat Trick

On October 8, 1995, Scott Mellanby of the Florida Panthers used his stick to kill a rat in the dressing room at the Miami Arena. That night, he scored two goals in a 4–3 win over the Calgary Flames. After the game, his teammates kidded him about scoring a "rat trick."

Newspapers reported the joke. After that, every time Mellanby scored a goal, fans threw rubber rats onto the ice. Soon, Florida fans were throwing rats on the ice whenever anyone on the team scored a goal. It seemed to bring the Panthers good luck. That season, the team went all the way to the Stanley Cup Finals.

NAME GAME

A committee chose the Philadelphia Flyers' name after 25,000 entries were sent in to a name-the-team contest. The child who submitted the winning entry had spelled Fliers correctly. But the "y" was taken from the word "Philly," which is what many people call Philadelphia for short.

A Real Lady's Man

Frank Boucher was a star player with the New York Rangers in the 1920s and '30s. Between 1928 and 1935, Boucher won the Lady Byng Trophy seven times in eight seasons. He won it so many times, the NHL gave him the original trophy to keep! Lady Byng donated a new one in 1936.

Masked Marvel

Jacques Plante was one of the best goalies in NHL history. He is also one of the most important. Plante was one of the first goalies to roam outside his crease. He would stop dump-ins behind his net, and he would get loose pucks in front and pass them to his defensemen. Most importantly, Jacques Plante made the goalie mask a standard piece of hockey equipment.

Before Jacques Plante, goalies faced shooters with a bare face. They were often cut and bruised. Some of them lost the sight in an eye after being hit in the face with a puck.

After surgery on his face during the 1957–58

Plante with his mask in a game against Toronto in 1959

season, Plante began wearing a mask in practice. The management of the Montreal Canadiens didn't want him using his mask in games, though. Then, on November 1, 1959, Plante was cut in the face by a shot from Andy Bathgate of the New York Rangers. At this time, NHL teams did not carry more than one goalie, so Plante had to get stitched up and go back into the game. But he refused to unless Canadiens coach Toe Blake let him wear his mask. Plante wore the mask, and the rest is history!

About Face

Although Jacques Plante made the goalie mask a standard piece of hockey equipment, he wasn't actually the first goalie to wear a mask in an NHL game. The first was Clint Benedict of the Montreal Maroons. He was hit in the face with shots in back-to-back games on January 4 and January 7, 1930. The second shot resulted in a badly broken nose. Benedict was sidelined for six weeks. When he returned to action on February 20, he wore a mask

made of leather. Benedict wore the mask for five games. Unfortunately, on the night of March 4, 1930, an Ottawa player fell on Benedict in a scramble. Benedict's mask pushed down on his face . . . and broke his nose again! Benedict never played another game in the NHL after that night.

But one of the earliest mentions of a goalie wearing a mask dates back more than 100 years. Eddie Giroux was a goalie with the Toronto Marlboros. During a pre-season practice in Toronto in December 1903, Giroux was hit in the face with a puck. To protect his injury, Giroux began to wear a baseball catcher's mask. Unfortunately, he had trouble following the puck through the bars of the mask. Giroux stopped wearing it before the season started.

The first goalie to wear a mask in an actual game is believed to be Elizabeth Graham. She played with a women's hockey team at Queen's University in Kingston, Ontario. Graham wore her mask in 1927 — three years before Clint Benedict wore his in the NHL. The *Montreal Daily Star*

reported that Graham "gave the fans a surprise when she stepped into the net and then donned a fencing mask."

According to stories, Elizabeth Graham's father pressured her into wearing the mask. He'd just paid for her to have expensive dental work.

The Next Six

Six more teams were added to the NHL during the 1970s. The Buffalo Sabres and Vancouver Canucks joined the league for the 1970–71 season. The Atlanta Flames and New York Islanders came along in 1972–73 and then, in 1974–75, the Washington Capitals and the Colorado Rockies. At first, Buffalo was the best of these new teams. It took the Sabres only five seasons to reach the Stanley Cup Finals, where they lost to Philadelphia in 1975. The New York Islanders started slowly, but they came on fast. They won the Stanley Cup in 1980 after just eight seasons in the league. Not only that, the Islanders went on to win the Cup for four years in a row!

DID YOU KNOW?

The record for most consecutive Stanley Cup Championships belongs to the Montreal Canadiens. The Habs won the Cup five years in a row from 1956 to 1960. Incredibly, they also won the Cup four years in a row from 1976 to 1979.

East is East, and West is . . . East?

Everyone knows that Vancouver is on Canada's west coast. Still, when the Canucks joined the NHL in 1970, they were put in the East Division and played there for four years. It seems strange, but the NHL thought having Vancouver in the East gave the divisions a better balance of old teams and expansion teams.

NAME GAME

Canucks was the name of a minor-league hockey team in Vancouver before the city got its NHL team in the 1970–71 season. Canuck is a slang term meaning Canadian. Another famous Canuck was Johnny Canuck, who was a Canadian comic strip hero during World War II.

50 in 50

By the start of the 1980–81 season, 35 years had
passed since Maurice Richard became hockey's first
50-goal-scorer. In that time, 23 more players had
scored 50 goals, and Phil Esposito had pushed the
scoring record all the way up to 76. Still, no one
but Maurice Richard had ever scored 50 goals in
just 50 games played.

During the 1980–81 season, two players were
scoring at a record rate: Mike Bossy of the New
York Islanders and Charlie Simmer of the Los
Angeles Kings. Bossy had scored 48 goals in 49
games while Simmer had 46 goals in 49 games. By
coincidence, both the Islanders and the Kings were
scheduled to play their 50th games on January 24,
1981. The Kings played Boston in the afternoon,
and the Islanders played the Quebec Nordiques that
night, which meant that Simmer got to play first.
There was a lot of pressure on him, and he sure
came close! He scored three goals that afternoon,
giving him 49 goals in 50 games.

Now the pressure was all on Bossy, and he was
struggling. Through two periods, he had yet to

score. Then, with only 4:10 to go in the game, he scored number 49. Bossy continued to get chances, but time was running out. Finally, with just 1:29 remaining, Bossy blasted the puck past Ron Grahame for his 50th of the season. Bossy and his teammates celebrated on the ice, as the scoreboard flashed "50! 50! 50! 50!" And Simmer? He scored his 50th two days later, in game number 51.

Bossy celebrates his 50th goal.

DID YOU KNOW?

Mike Bossy was the first player in NHL history to score 50 goals in his rookie season. He did it with 53 goals for the Islanders in 1977–78.

NAME GAME

The Calgary Flames began life as the Atlanta Flames in 1972–73. The name Flames was chosen to commemorate the rebirth of the city after the burning of Atlanta during the American Civil War. When the Flames moved to Calgary in the 1980–81 season, fans got to vote on the name. They decided to keep the name Flames.

The Great One

Wayne Gretzky was born to be a hockey star. He had already learned to skate by the time he was two years old. Soon after that, his father built a rink in the backyard of their house, where Gretzky liked to skate for hours. By the time he was six years old, he was playing on a hockey team with boys who were 10. When he was 10, Gretzky scored 378 goals in a single season.

Gretzky signed his first professional hockey contract when he was just 17 years old. Players that young are not allowed to play in the NHL. Instead, he signed with a new rival league called the World Hockey Association. Although he played with men much older than he was, Gretzky was one of the WHA's top scorers.

The next year, in 1979–80, four WHA teams joined the NHL. Gretzky's Edmonton Oilers was one of those four teams. People believed that Gretzky wouldn't do as well in the NHL as he had in the WHA. They thought he was too young and too small to succeed. Were they ever wrong! In his first season, Gretzky scored 51 goals. He also had 86 assists for a total of 137 points. Although these totals would have been rookie records, Gretzky's season in the WHA meant he didn't qualify as an NHL rookie.

In his second NHL season, Gretzky got 109 assists, breaking Bobby Orr's record of 102 in a single year. Combined with his 55 goals, that gave him 164 points to break Phil Esposito's record of 152. Over the years, Gretzky would continue to break records. He pushed the assist mark from 109 to 120 to 125 to 135, then finally to 163. No one has ever broken that record. Gretzky also pushed the points record from 164 all the way to 215, a record that still stands to this day. Not bad for someone who was too young and too small.

Gretzky bids an emotional farewell at his final game in New York

DID YOU KNOW?

Team captains have been part of hockey since the game's earliest days. In 1946 the NHL enacted Rule 14a, which required the captain to wear a "C" on the front of his uniform. Alternate captains are required to wear an "A." The captain or alternate captains are the only players on the ice who are allowed to talk to the referee.

NAME GAME

When Edmonton got its WHA team, management held a contest to choose a name. Oilers was chosen to reflect the importance of the oil industry in Alberta. Back in the 1950s, Edmonton also had a great junior hockey team known as the Edmonton Oil Kings.

BY THE NUMBERS

Wayne Gretzky has won the Hart Trophy as the NHL's Most Valuable Player more times than anyone else in history. Here is a list of players who have won the Hart Trophy the most times:

Player	Wins
Wayne Gretzky	9
Gordie Howe	6
Eddie Shore	4
Mario Lemieux	3
Bobby Clarke	3
Bobby Orr	3
Howie Morenz	3

DID YOU KNOW?

Not just anyone is allowed to be a team captain. Although few NHL teams have ever had a playing coach, if they ever do, that player is not allowed to be a captain. And goalies aren't allowed to be captains, either. That rule (Rule 14d) was passed in 1948. People thought it would delay the game too much for a goalie to leave his crease to discuss things with the referee. Before this rule was passed, six different NHL goalies had served as captains of their team. The last one was Bill Durnan of the Montreal Canadiens. He wore the "C" during the 1947–48 season.

BY THE NUMBERS

Here's a look at some of the top single-season goal scorers in NHL history:

Goals	Player	Team	Season
92	Wayne Gretzky	Edmonton	1981–82
87	Wayne Gretzky	Edmonton	1983–84
86	Brett Hull	St. Louis	1990–91
85	Mario Lemieux	Pittsburgh	1988–89
76	Phil Esposito	Boston	1970–71
76	Alexander Mogilny	Buffalo	1992–93
76	Teemu Selanne	Winnipeg	1992–93
73	Wayne Gretzky	Edmonton	1984–85

D'oh!

Wayne Gretzky played in 49 different arenas during his NHL career. He had at least one point in 48 of them. Which arena saw Gretzky go pointless? The Springfield Civic Center. The Civic Center in Springfield, Massachusetts, was the home of the Hartford Whalers for the first four months of the 1979–80 season. After that, the Whalers moved back to the Civic Center in Hartford, Connecticut.

Gretzky's 50

In 1981–82, Wayne Gretzky smashed the marks of Maurice Richard and Mike Bossy for 50 goals in 50 games. On December 30, 1981, in just his 39th game, Gretzky scored his 50th goal of the season: he'd scored five goals that night to break the record. But Gretzky didn't stop there. He went on to break Phil Esposito's single-season record of 76 goals. He did that in his 64th game on February 24, 1982, when he scored three goals. Gretzky continued to push the record all the way up to 92 goals. Like his records for points and assists, no one has broken Gretzky's goal-scoring record either.

DID YOU KNOW?

The longest winning streak and the longest losing streak in NHL history both lasted 17 games. Two different teams have had losing streaks of 17 in a row. The first was the Washington Capitals, who lost 17 straight from February 18 to March 26, 1975. Then, in 1993, the San Jose Sharks lost 17 in a row from January 4 to February 12. As for the longest winning streak? That belongs to the Pittsburgh Penguins, who won 17 straight games from March 9 to April 10, 1993.

CUP CAPERS

In 1986 Chris Nilan of the Montreal Canadiens took a picture of his baby son sitting inside the Stanley Cup bowl. "His bottom fit right in," said the noted hockey tough guy. He started a trend. In 1996 Colorado Avalanche defenseman Sylvain Lefebvre christened his new baby in the bowl of the Cup.

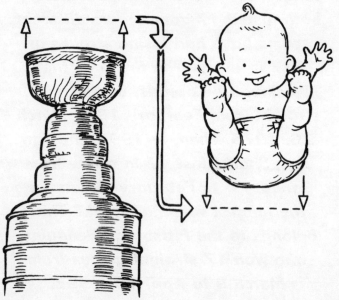

NAME GAME

The Tampa Bay Lightning entered the NHL for the 1992–93 season. The name Lightning was chosen for the team because of the many violent thunderstorms in the Tampa Bay area. The city of Tampa is known as the lightning capital of the United States.

Captain Kid

Vincent Lecavalier was named captain of the Tampa Bay Lightning on March 3, 2000. At the time, he was just 19 years and 11 months old. That made Lecavalier the youngest captain in NHL history. However, after the 2000–01 season, the Lightning took the "C" away. They decided that being such a young captain put too much pressure on Lecavalier. Maybe they were right. Lecavalier has become a star player since.

NAME GAME

Columbus played its first NHL season in 2000–01. The name Blue Jackets was chosen to commemorate the pride and patriotism of the state of Ohio during the American Civil War. During that war, Ohio had contributed more of its population to the Union Army than any other state, and the soldiers who joined the Union Army wore blue jackets. In addition, many of those blue Civil War jackets were actually made right in Columbus.

Rookie Rewards

The NHL has been rewarding its Rookie of the Year since 1933. From 1937 until his death in 1943, NHL president Frank Calder would buy a new trophy every year. After his death, the NHL presented a permanent trophy, which they named the Calder Memorial Trophy.

Lucky Number

Sidney Crosby wears number 87 because of his birthday, which is August 7. That's the eighth month and the seventh day. And what year was he born? 1987, of course.

NAME GAME

Washington joined the NHL for the 1974–75 season. The name Capitals was picked for the team because Washington is the capital city of the United States.

CUP CAPERS

The Montreal Canadiens won the Stanley Cup four years in a row from 1976 to 1979. Back then, players on the winning team didn't get to spend a day with the Cup as they do now.

After the traditional Stanley Cup

parade in 1979, star forward Guy Lafleur grabbed the prized trophy. He stuck it in the trunk of his car and drove to his parents' house in Thurso, Quebec. When he got there, he displayed the Cup on the front lawn. Friends and family stopped by to see the trophy and take pictures.

While the people in Thurso were having fun, the people in Montreal who were responsible for the Cup's safety were frantic. They didn't know where the Cup had gone. When Lafleur returned it later that night, he was told never to repeat his stunt again.

Mario the Magnificent

Mario Lemieux was a star player. He was chosen first overall by the Pittsburgh Penguins in the 1984 draft, and quickly helped make the team one of the best in the league. In just his second season, he finished second behind Wayne Gretzky in the league scoring race. Even after suffering a serious back injury in the 1989–90 season, he led the Penguins to their first Stanley Cup Championship. But then on January 12, 1993, the Penguins announced that Mario had Hodgkin's Disease, a form of cancer. He had to leave the team to get therapy.

Lemieux's cancer treatments — which are very tiring — lasted from February 1 to March 2. But on the very day he finished his treatment, Lemieux returned to action with the Penguins.

Before getting sick, Lemieux had collected 104 points in just 40 games. He was 20 points in front in the NHL scoring race. However, he'd missed 20 games while he was sick. By March 7, Pat LaFontaine, Adam Oates and Steve Yzerman had all passed him in the scoring race. LaFontaine was the leader now, and he was 16 points ahead of Lemieux.

Sick as he'd been, no one expected that Lemieux could possibly catch up. But he did. Lemieux scored 30 goals and got 26 assists in the last 20 games of the season. He finished the year with just 60 games played, but had 69 goals and 91 assists for 160 points. LaFontaine, Oates and Yzerman had each played 24 more games than Lemieux, but he had passed them all. Lemieux won the race for the Art Ross Trophy by 12 points. And once again, he won the Hart Trophy.

Lemieux with the Stanley Cup

NAME GAME

In the 1912–13 season, two Toronto teams joined the National Hockey Assocation: the Toronto Tecumsehs and the Toronto Blueshirts. The Blueshirts were often just called the Torontos.

When the NHL was formed, control of the Toronto team was given to the Toronto Arena Company. So Toronto's first NHL team was known as the Toronto Arenas. In 1920, the team became known as the Toronto St. Patricks.

In February 1927 Conn Smythe bought the team. Smythe changed the team's name to the Toronto Maple Leafs for a couple of reasons. One was that the 1924 Canadian Olympic hockey team had worn a maple leaf on its sweaters. The other was that Canadian soldiers fighting in World War I had worn maple leaf insignias on their uniforms.

CUP CAPERS

After winning the Stanley Cup in 1991, Mario Lemieux hosted a victory party for the Penguins. During the party, the Stanley Cup got tossed in Lemieux's swimming pool. It sank to the bottom before it was rescued!

DID YOU KNOW?

Gus Bodnar holds the record for the fastest goal from the start of an NHL career. Bodnar scored just 15 seconds after the opening face-off in his first NHL game. The goal came for the Toronto Maple Leafs versus the New York Rangers on October 30, 1943.

Saturday Night is Hockey Night

Hockey Night in Canada is the longest-running show on Canadian television. The Canadian Broadcasting Corporation (CBC) first showed a hockey game on TV on Saturday, October 11, 1952, between the Detroit Red Wings and the Montreal Canadiens.

The Toronto Maple Leafs made their first appearance on *Hockey Night in Canada* three weeks later, on November 1, 1952.

Huselius Hat Trick

Though he's now a member of the Calgary Flames, Kristian Huselius began his career with the Florida Panthers with his own unique version of a hat trick. In the first game of the 2001–02 season, Huselius scored the first goal of his career on his very first shot in the NHL. A year later, he did it again: he scored a goal on his very first shot in the very first game of the 2002–03 season. He made it three in a row in 2003–04 when he once again scored a goal on his first shot of the season! That was the end of his first-game scoring streak, though. However, in his first game for Calgary in 2005–06, Huselius did pick up three assists.

NAME GAME

The NHL added a team in Miami, Florida, in 1993. Original team owner Wayne Huizenga wanted to draw attention to the panther, which is an endangered native wildcat of Florida, so he decided to call the team the Florida Panthers.

On The Air

Most people think that Foster Hewitt was the first person to broadcast a hockey game on the radio. He wasn't. The first person was a man named Norman Albert.

Both Albert and Hewitt worked for the *Toronto Star*. During the 1920s and '30s, the *Star* owned a Toronto radio station called CFCA. Foster Hewitt did work for the radio station, but Albert was a sports reporter with the newspaper. When CFCA decided to broadcast a hockey game on the radio for the first time, on February 8, 1923, they chose Albert to call the play-by-play. The game was an amateur playoff between North Toronto and Midland.

CFCA broadcast the first NHL game on the radio six days later. It was a game between the Ottawa Senators and Toronto St. Patricks. Though it's not known for sure, Albert was probably the broadcaster that night too.

Foster's First

When Foster Hewitt talked about his first radio broadcast, he always said that it was on March 22, 1923. He usually said that it was a semifinal playoff game between the Kitchener Greenshirts and the Parkdale Canoe Club of Toronto. The winner would face the Toronto Granites in the Eastern Canada final.

 But there are two problems with Foster Hewitt's story. First, Kitchener and Parkdale never played a game that night. Second, by March 22, 1923, the Toronto Granites had already won the amateur championship.

Later in his life, Foster Hewitt admitted that his memory of the two teams might have been wrong. "I know Kitchener played," he said. "But it may well have been against the Toronto Argonauts." (Back then, the Toronto Argonauts had an amateur hockey team as well as a Canadian football team.)

It turns out that the Toronto Argonauts played a hockey game against the Kitchener Greenshirts on February 16, 1923. This is the game where Foster Hewitt made his first broadcast. His call of the play-by-play was so popular that he soon became a full-time radio sports announcer.

Foster Hewitt lived from 1902 to 1985, but he is probably still the most famous sports broadcaster in Canadian history.

Radio Days

CFCA broadcasts in 1923 only covered the third period and any overtime periods. The first radio station to carry a complete hockey broadcast was CJCG in Winnipeg. That station aired all 60 minutes of an amateur playoff game between the Winnipeg Falcons and the Port Arthur Bearcats on February 22, 1923.

CKCK in Regina was the first radio station to broadcast a full professional hockey game, on March 14, 1923. The game was the first of a Western Canada Hockey League playoff series between the Regina Capitals and the Edmonton Eskimos.

NAME GAME

Anaheim entered the NHL for the 1993–94 season. Originally, the Walt Disney Company owned the team, and one of their movies, *The Mighty Ducks*, was popular at the time. So Disney used that name for their team.

CUP CAPERS

The Ottawa Senators won the Stanley Cup four times in the 1920s: 1920, 1921, 1923 and 1927. After winning the Cup in 1923, King Clancy brought the Cup home to show his father.

The next season, NHL president Frank Calder asked the Senators to return the Cup. The problem was, none of the team executives could find it! It was then that Clancy admitted the Stanley Cup was still at his house, sitting on his mantel.

DID YOU KNOW?

During the 1990s, many northern-based teams moved south. Teams in Minnesota, Quebec, Winnipeg and Hartford moved to Dallas, Colorado, Phoenix and Carolina. When the NHL had 21 teams, 7 were in Canada and 14 were in the United States. Now that the NHL has 30 teams, only 6 are in Canada.

NAME GAME

Before moving to Dallas in 1993, the team was based in the city of Minneapolis. Since Minnesota is one of the northernmost states in the United States, and its state motto is *Étoile du Nord* — Star of the North — they called their team the Minnesota North Stars. The southern state of Texas is known as the Lone Star State. It was a simple decision to drop the word North from the name and call the team the Dallas Stars.

CUP CAPERS

Since 1995, each member of the Stanley Cup-winning team has been allowed to spend one special day with the prized trophy. It makes for a busy summer of travel. Usually everything goes smoothly . . . but not always.

On August 23, 2004, the Hockey Hall of Fame employee who delivers the Cup got off a plane in the small town of Fort St. John in northern British Columbia. He was supposed to deliver the Stanley Cup to Jake Goertzen, head scout for the Tampa Bay Lightning. He waited patiently for his special container to be unloaded from the luggage compartment. But the container never arrived. Turns out that the airplane had been full and that the 16-kilogram Stanley Cup had been removed because it was too heavy. It spent the night in the luggage area of the Vancouver airport, some 1,200 kilometres away. It arrived safely the next morning.

Edmonton On Ice

On November 22, 2003, the NHL staged its first outdoor hockey game. The "Heritage Classic" was held in Edmonton, Alberta. It was played on a rink built inside the city's football field, Commonwealth Stadium. At game time, the temperature in Edmonton was –18.6 degrees Celsius. That didn't stop diehard fans — the crowd that night swelled to 57,167, shattering the all-time NHL attendance record. They watched the Montreal Canadiens beat the Oilers 4–3.

On The Move

After missing a whole season in 2004–05, more than 200 NHL players changed teams when the lockout ended. Every team in the NHL had new faces in training camp . . . except one. The San Jose Sharks did not add a single new player from outside their organization.

Rules to Live By

Even before the NHL lockout, many fans were complaining that games had become too boring. There was too much clutching and grabbing, and there wasn't enough scoring.

When the league came back in 2005–06, many rules were changed to try to open up the game. Goalies were forced to wear smaller equipment, and referees were told to call more penalties. Passing rules were also changed. Players could now pass the puck all the way from their own end up to the other team's blue line.

One of the biggest changes to the rules was the introduction of the shootout. If games are still tied after playing one overtime period, players now take penalty shots to decide the winner. Three players shoot for each team, but if the game is still tied after that, players keep shooting until there is a winner. The team that wins gets two points in the standings. The team that loses gets one.

Ottawa Shoots to Victory

The NHL's first shootout occurred on the very first night of the 2005–06 season. After three periods of play, Ottawa and Toronto ended in a 2–2 tie. When overtime didn't decide it, the game went to a shootout.

Martin Havlat became the first player in NHL history to score a shootout goal, and Dany Heatley clinched the victory with another goal for Ottawa after Toronto was unable to score.

Game Seven and Then Some

Only twice in NHL history has the seventh game of the Stanley Cup Finals gone into overtime, and the Detroit Red Wings won both. In 1950 Detroit beat the New York Rangers 4–3. Pete Babando scored the winning goal at 8:31 of the second overtime period. The hero in 1954 was Tony Leswick. His goal at 4:29 of overtime gave Detroit a 2–1 win over the Montreal Canadiens.

NAME GAME

The name Devils for New Jersey's hockey team was chosen from an old legend about a half-man, half-beast that roams the New Jersey countryside.

BY THE NUMBERS

A total of 15 players have scored the Stanley Cup-winning goal in overtime.

Bill Cook, New York Rangers	1933 (Game Four)
Mush March, Chicago Black Hawks	1934 (Game Four, 2OT)
Bryan Hextall, New York Rangers	1940 (Game Six, 2OT)
Toe Blake, Montreal Canadiens	1944 (Game Four)
Pete Babando, Detroit Red Wings	1950 (Game Seven, 2OT)
Bill Barilko, Toronto Maple Leafs	1951 (Game Five)
Elmer Lach, Montreal Canadiens	1953 (Game Five)
Tony Leswick, Detroit Red Wings	1954 (Game Seven)

Henri Richard,
Montreal Canadiens   1966 (Game Six)

Bobby Orr,
Boston Bruins   1970 (Game Four)

Jacques Lemaire,
Montreal Canadiens   1977 (Game Four)

Bob Nystrom,
New York Islanders   1980 (Game Six)

Uwe Krupp,
Colorado Avalanche   1996 (Game Four, 3OT)

Brett Hull,
Dallas Stars   1999 (Game Six, 3OT)

Jason Arnott,
New Jersey Devils   2000 (Game Six, 2OT)

DID YOU KNOW?

Patrick Roy has more wins than any other goalie in NHL history. He is the career leader in the regular season with 551 wins and the career leader in playoff wins with 151 wins.

Roy with the Cup in 1993

By George!

The award given to the NHL's best goalie is called the Vezina Trophy. It's named in honour of Georges Vezina who was a star goalie with the Montreal Canadiens in the 1910s and '20s. Vezina joined the Canadiens for the 1910–11 season. For the next 15 years, he never missed a single game, regular season or playoffs. His streak got up to 367 games. Then, on November 28, 1925, Vezina missed a game due to a pain in his chest. It turned out the pain was caused by tuberculosis, a very serious lung disease. Sadly, he died four months later. In memory of him, the owners of the Canadiens presented the Vezina Trophy to the NHL for the 1926–27 season.

He Shoots,
He . . . Flies?

The Boston Bruins had not won the Stanley Cup for
29 years. Then, in 1970, Bobby Orr won the series
with an overtime goal. He lifted the puck past St.
Louis goalie Glenn Hall just as Blues defenseman
Noel Picard tripped him. Orr flew through the air
with his arms raised in triumph and a big smile on
his face. The picture of Orr celebrating his goal is
one of the most famous images in hockey history.

Number four, Bobby Orr!

The Vezina Trophy used to be awarded to the goalie (or goalies) on the team that allowed the fewest goals. The rules were changed for the 1981–82 season. That year, it was decided that the Vezina Trophy should go to the goalie who was voted to be the best in the league. A new trophy was donated to reward the goalies on the team that gives up the fewest goals. That trophy is the William Jennings Trophy. Jennings was president of the New York Rangers and helped popularize hockey in the United States.

BY THE NUMBERS

Here's a look at the goalies who have won the Vezina Trophy the most times:

Goalie	Wins
Jacques Plante	7
Dominik Hasek	6
Bill Durnan	6
Ken Dryden	5
Michel Laroque	4
Terry Sawchuk	4
Tiny Thompson	4
Patrick Roy	3
Glenn Hall	3
George Hainsworth	3

George, the Sequel

After the death of Georges Vezina, George
Hainsworth became the Montreal Canadiens'
goaltender. And he was a good one! He won the
Vezina Trophy the first three years it was presented.
At that time, forward passing was not allowed in
the offensive zone. Players trying to score could
only shoot, stickhandle the puck or drop-pass it to
someone, which gave goalies a big advantage.

During the 1928–29 season, Hainsworth set
a record for shutouts that is not likely ever to be
beaten. The season was just 44 games long that
year, and he had 22 shutouts. He only let 43 shots
get past him all season. His goals-against average
was 0.92. The next year, the NHL changed its rules
and allowed players to pass the puck forward from
anywhere on the ice.

DID YOU KNOW?

In 1907 the Kenora Thistles from Ontario became the team from the smallest town ever to win the Stanley Cup. The town's population in 1907 was only about 6,000. Kenora also had hockey's shortest reign as Stanley Cup champions. They won the Cup in January 1907, but were defeated in a challenge match for the trophy that March.

CUP CAPERS

To try to win their series in March 1907, the Kenora Thistles made two late additions to their lineup. When a Stanley Cup trustee refused to let them use these players, a Kenora official is said to have threatened to throw the Cup into the Lake of the Woods. He didn't . . . but Kenora did get to use the two players!

NAME GAME

Fans selected the name Nashville Predators in a name-the-team contest. Club president Craig Leipold thought the name made sense for a sport that combined speed and skill. For a logo, the Predators chose a sabre-toothed cat. This ice-age mammal had been native to the area.

Cherry and Grapes

With his loud suits and even louder opinions, Don Cherry has become one of the most famous people in hockey. Love him or hate him, people tune in to Coach's Corner on *Hockey Night in Canada* just to see what he has to say.

The Boston Bruins signed Don Cherry in 1952. He played hockey until 1972, but he only ever got into one game in the NHL — a playoff game in 1955. He was a coach in the NHL from 1974 until 1980, mostly with the Bruins. He's been a TV commentator since then.

Cherry is known by the nickname "Grapes." Cherry actually got the nickname while playing minor league hockey with the Springfield Indians. Springfield owner Eddie Shore used to pay off the fines for players he liked, but he didn't like Cherry, so he wouldn't pay his fines. When Cherry got mad at another player and called him a name, Shore said, "Ah, that's just sour grapes," meaning that Cherry was just complaining. Soon, though, the rest of his teammates were calling him "Grapes" and the name stuck.

Cherry on the set of *Hockey Night in Canada* with co-host Ron MacLean

Maple Leaf Forever

Every year since 1965, the person who is voted the Most Valuable Player in the playoffs has received the Conn Smythe Trophy. This trophy was presented to the NHL in 1964 by the management of Maple Leaf Gardens. It honours Conn Smythe, a man who served as coach, manager, president, owner and governor of the Toronto Maple Leafs (sometimes all at the same time!) from 1927 to 1961. Smythe was also responsible for building Maple Leaf Gardens in 1931. That's why the Conn Smythe Trophy looks like Maple Leaf Gardens.

BY THE NUMBERS

Terry Sawchuk, who played 21 seasons in the NHL and played more games than any other goalie, has had his record for career wins passed by Patrick Roy and by Ed Belfour. Still, Sawchuk's record for regular-season career shutouts should be safe. Here's a look at the NHL's top 10 shutout leaders:

Goalie	Seasons	Games	Shutouts
Terry Sawchuk	20	971	103
George Hainsworth	11	465	94
Glenn Hall	18	906	84
Jacques Plante	18	837	82
Tiny Thompson	12	553	81
Alex Connell	12	417	81
Martin Brodeur	12	740	80
Ed Belfour	15	856	75
Tony Esposito	16	886	76
Lorne Chabot	11	411	72

In Memory

Maurice Richard was more than just a hockey hero. He was an idol to people all across Quebec. When he died in Montreal on May 27, 2000, even people who had never seen him play were saddened.

To allow his fans to pay their last respects, Maurice Richard's body lay in state at the Molson Centre, the home rink of the Canadiens (now called the Bell Centre). More than 115,000 people filed past to say goodbye. On May 31, 2000, funeral services were held at the Notre-Dame Basilica, once the biggest church in North America.

Years earlier, another Montreal hockey hero had been paid a similar tribute. Howie Morenz was the biggest star in hockey in the 1920s and '30s. On January 28, 1937, Morenz suffered a badly broken leg in an on-ice collision at the Montreal Forum. He died in hospital on March 8, 1937.

Morenz's funeral was held March 11 at centre ice in the Forum. About 12,000 people attended. Almost that many stood outside the building to pay tribute. Thousands more lined the streets en route to the cemetery in order to pay their last respects.

The Zamboni Man

Zamboni is not just the name of the machine that cleans the ice at hockey games. It's the name of the man who invented it . . . Frank J. Zamboni.

Frank J. Zamboni was born on January 16, 1901, in Eureka, Utah. In 1920 he and his younger brother Lawrence went to California to work for their older brother George, who operated a garage in the twin cities of Hynes-Clearwater.

In 1927 Frank and Lawrence Zamboni built a factory that made blocks of ice. This ice was used in iceboxes, which were an early type of refrigerator.

The first Zamboni

By 1939 better brands of refrigerators meant that ice was in less demand. So, in 1940, Frank, Lawrence and cousin Pete Zamboni opened a skating rink. At the time, resurfacing the ice in skating rinks meant pulling a scraper behind a tractor to shave the surface. Three or four workers would scoop away the shavings, spray water over the surface, squeegee it clean and allow the water to freeze. The whole process took more than an hour. Frank began to wonder how he could he make a better sheet of ice in a shorter period of time. He started experimenting with a tractor in 1942, and by 1949, he had a design that he liked. Though he would continue to make improvements to his machine over the years, the Zamboni was born.

Then, in 1950, a famous figure skater, Sonja Henie, saw Frank's new machine. She ordered a Zamboni for her ice show in Chicago. In 1954 the Boston Bruins bought a Zamboni for the Boston Garden. Soon, every team in the NHL had a Zamboni for their arena. And they still do today.

Series of the Century

In the early days of hockey history, Canada was always the best at international competitions. Professional players were not allowed to compete at tournaments like the Olympics, but from the 1920s until the 1950s, Canada could send a top amateur team from anywhere in the country and expect to come home with a gold medal.

As the years went by, Canada's amateurs could no longer keep up. During the 1960s the Soviet Union began to dominate. International games still did not allow NHL players, so Canada's best stars could never face the Soviets. Finally, arrangements were made for a special eight-game "Summit Series" in 1972. There would be four games in Canadian cities followed by four games in Moscow.

Most Canadians expected an easy victory for their NHL stars. They were stunned when the Soviets won the series opener in Montreal 7–3.

Team Canada won the second game in Toronto 4–1. Then, as there was no overtime in the series, there was a 4–4 tie in Winnipeg. Next came another loss, this time 5–3, in Vancouver. People all across the country were disappointed in their team. Many fans at the Vancouver game booed the Canadians.

When the series resumed in Moscow, the Soviets won again. Canada had been up 4–1 in the game, but lost 5–4. Now the Soviets led the series three games to one with one game tied. Canada would have to win all three remaining games to win the series. It seemed like an impossible goal, but they did it. In each game, Paul Henderson scored the winning goal. Game eight was the most dramatic of all. Canada was trailing 5–3 after two periods. Early

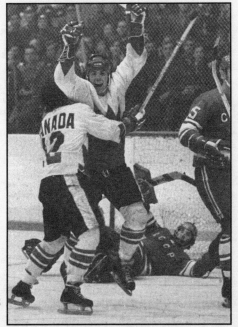

Henderson celebrates his game-winning goal.

in the third, Phil Esposito scored to make it 5–4. Midway through the period, he set up Yvon Cournoyer with the tying goal. Then, with just 34 seconds left in the game, Henderson scored again. Canada had won the series!

After more than thirty years, the series is still remembered as the most dramatic of all time.

Good As Gold

After 1972 more and more professional players were allowed to play at international tournaments. Still, it wasn't until 1998 that active NHL players could compete at the Winter Olympics. When the Canadian men's team won the gold medal at Salt Lake City in 2002, it marked the first time in 50 years that Canada had won the Olympic gold medal in hockey. In fact, Canadian hockey players won two gold medals in 2002. The women's team also won the Olympic Championship that year and followed it with another gold medal at the 2006 Winter Olympics.

Cancelled Cup

When the NHL lockout cancelled the 2004–05 hockey season, it marked just the second time since 1893 that a hockey season had ended without a Stanley Cup champion. The only other time was in 1919. During 1918 and 1919, a very serious flu epidemic, commonly referred to as the Spanish Flu, spread around the world. Millions of people died.

In March 1919 the Montreal Canadiens were facing the Seattle Metropolitans in the Stanley Cup Final. It was a gruelling series, with two long overtime games. As the series stretched on, several Canadiens players got sick. The final game of the series was scheduled for April 1, but so many players were suffering from the flu that the game had to be cancelled. There would be no Stanley Cup champion for 1919.

Sadly, Canadiens star Joe Hall was so sick that he died on April 5, 1919. Canadiens owner George Kennedy never fully recovered from his bout with the flu. He died in October 1920.

Surprise Attack

When teams pulled their goalies during the 1930s, they always did it during a stop in play. But New York Rangers coach Frank Boucher thought it would give him an advantage if he pulled his goalie while play was going on. He tried it for the first time on January 14, 1940. The Rangers had gone 19 games in a row without a loss. They were going for number 20, but they were losing to Chicago 2–1.

At the end of the second period, Boucher told goalie Dave Kerr that if the Rangers were still trailing by one late in the game he was going to pull him. He told him he wasn't going to wait for a stop and that Kerr should watch for a signal. Boucher gave Kerr the signal with about 1:30 remaining in the game. The move certainly caught everyone by surprise, but it didn't work. The Rangers lost. Their streak was over, but hockey had a brand-new tactic.